changing

images

Photography, Education and Young People

By Jane Brake

Edited by
Darren Newbury

Contents

Viewpoint Photography Gallery and Artbase Studios

Salford City Council

The Old Fire Station

The Crescent

Salford

M5 4NZ

Tel: (0161) 737 1040

Fax: (0161) 736 0429

First published in 1996 by Viewpoint Photography Gallery

Design: Alan Ward & Chris Wilcock @ Axis

Printed by Jackson Wilson, Leeds

© Viewpoint Photography Gallery

ISBN 0 901952 91 5

Map reproduction page 58:

© Crown copyright, Ordnance Survey

Cover image: Video still, Time Capsule 2045,

Ellen Wilkinson High School, Chen Chuong

Acknowledgements

This book is the result of many partnerships. Without the hard work, commitment, and faith in the project demonstrated by many individuals, this book could never have been conceived. I am grateful to colleagues in the Centre for Art and Design Education at Manchester Metropolitan University for believing in the project from the outset. In particular I would like to thank the other members of the project team, Pat Procter and Keith Walker for their support and insights throughout my time at the university, and also for permission to adapt their material about the project at Grange School originally published in the Journal of Art and Design Education. Thanks also to the National Society for Education in Art and Design for allowing us to include a revised version of that article in this publication.

It is also appropriate at this point to say a few words about the process of writing. In the spirit of collaboration that underpins all the material in this book, its construction too is not the work of a single authorial voice. In a process of making that is itself a creative activity, the editor, Darren Newbury, constructed the final form of the publication from the plethora of raw material generated by each of the projects, and from my own written accounts. The intention was not to fit the many voices present in each project to a single pattern, but rather to build a constructive dialogue between artists, teachers, researchers and students. I am grateful to Darren for his skill in achieving this and for ensuring I kept on top of all the deadlines.

I am endebted to Viv Reiss from the Arts Council of England for her support for the project as a whole and for the publication in particular, many thanks to her. My appreciation to Jo Booth, Rebecca Sinker, Angela Rogers and Terry Taylor and the other post holders, conversations during and after our meetings have informed this book in many ways. I am grateful to the other members of the project steering group: Richard Andrews, Aileen McEvoy, Janet Matthewman and Tony Woof for their useful contributions throughout the project and for their role in helping shape the concept of this book. Thanks to Oldham Art Gallery for their contribution to the project at Grange School, and to Lee Avison for running the workshop for students in the gallery. I am grateful to Michael Elphick for his help with photographic documentation of several of the projects. Thanks to Emma Anderson from North West Arts Board for her support in values which need to be engaged in education, but which defeat students' contemporaneous abilities in other forms of articulation and communication, principally verbal and graphic. Images in this book 'speak' profoundly of students' innermost conceptions of self and identity; of origins and destinies; of the intangible characteristics of places which distinguish them from all other, ostensibly similar, places; and of the intimate connections between place and time. The profundity in these evocations is regarded as exceptional if and when it is achieved by other means, but here it becomes apparent that precise communication of deep and complex mixtures of feelings and thoughts is achievable by all. This is possibly the main reason why advocates of photography in education are so despondent about its present neglect. What is being disregarded is a medium which enables students to express their inner feelings and thoughts without predisposition - to work in a way that is driven by feeling, to encapsulate their feelings in images, and to interrogate their images thoughtfully so that their feelings are made tangible to themselves as well as to others.

The second principle which is revealed in this work is that experience of producing photographic imagery makes students far less vulnerable to the subtle manipulation of visual information in their staple consumption of photographs in both education and the culture at large. Especially if students are encouraged to use the medium in all its spontaneity, accepting the often ill-matched nature of film speed, camera format and ambient conditions, they will be naturally wary of images which are so pristine that they smack of artifice. If students are encouraged to experiment with superimposition and projection, with collaging and cropping, they are likely to realise that messages in the wider photographic culture are routinely modified in such ways. In other words, their general consumption of images will be informed by a 'practitioner critique'. It would be a failing education which neglected to provide its recipients with practitioner insights into word or number. It is a failing education which deprives students of insider knowledge and experience of the most sophisticated communication medium of the modern world.

The selection of curricular interventions in this book exposes a fundamental misapprehension - namely that photography is a surrogate for 'real' experience. This work demonstrates its creative and synthetic nature: it enables students to reflect on both internal and external realms, and thus to interrelate the personal, the social and the environmental. It is not unique in this: art and design and creative writing have similar propensities. Photography, however, is a direct and immediate extension of sensation and perception. No complicated conjectural or motorial skills are required for students to begin working, with profundity and sophistication, in and with the culture at large. Conjectural, motorial and a host of other attributes ensue as a result. Photography crosses all subject boundaries and key stages of percipient development. What more genuinely educational medium could there possibly be?

David Thistlewood, Professor in History of Art, University of Liverpool

Introduction

Changing Images is the culmination of a three-year photography in education development project set up by the Arts Council of England in collaboration with Manchester Metropolitan University and Viewpoint Photography Gallery in Salford. It brings together four case studies of extended photography in education projects that took place in schools in Greater Manchester between 1994 and 1996. The book looks at a range of ideas and innovative practices through the focused lens of complex 'real-time' case studies, highlighting the exciting and challenging ways in which photographic work can contribute to the curriculum (in particular at Key Stage 4). Throughout the book equal weight is given to the different 'voices' that have contributed to the projects: teachers, students and artists. Equally important, the photographic and visual work produced by the students is presented as worthy of consideration in its own right, and not merely as illustration for the written text. The purpose of this introduction is to place the case studies in the context of the educational and cultural debates that have informed their development, and to highlight issues and ideas of particular importance.

This publication comes at an opportune moment in the development of photography in education for two reasons. First, the fact that photography, along with media work, has retained its position in the revised National Curriculum orders suggests that the arguments for its educational significance have been successful. The principle of the importance of educational work in relation to contemporary visual and media culture has broad acceptance across most quarters of the education sector. This is due in large part to the work of the Arts Council of England in supporting innovative research and practice, and not least to the publication of *Creating Vision: Photography and the National Curriculum* [1]. This does not mean, however, that it is time for advocates of photography to sit back and congratulate themselves, indeed precisely opposite is the case. There has perhaps been no better opportunity for open debate and new curriculum initiatives in photography in the last ten years. Only a few years ago photography educators were continually in the position of having to argue the case for photography's inclusion, even within the art curriculum. Although in many instances this is still the case, with the importance of photography and media work now established at a national level, new opportunities exist. However, without proper guidance and models of practice to inspire teachers in schools it is unlikely that photography work will develop to the extent that is now possible. It is time to leave the neatness of theories of photography in education and engage the complexities of practice. An absence of exemplars would result in photography work remaining trapped within the orthodoxies of a formulaic art education, which fails to engage the cultural knowledge and imagination of young people. Although the inclusion of photography in the National Curriculum orders for Art is a necessary condition of the development of photography in education, it is not a sufficient one. The orders for art do little to encourage or reward innovation. It is in support of new initiatives in photography and media education that this publication is aimed.

The second reason why this publication comes at an opportune time is that the photographic and media industries are entering a period of rapid and significant technological development. Photography is rapidly shifting from the chemical base that has served the last 150 years, to a predominantly electronic one. This has many important implications for the way in which we make sense of, and use, images. Notwithstanding the more effusive journalistic and critical attention that they have attracted, new technologies are not a good thing in themselves. Any proper assessment of their importance must consider the social, cultural and political contexts in which they are used and understood. However, for educators in photography such changes do provide a window of opportunity. Over the coming years the resources available in schools for work with computing technology are likely to increase significantly. Where there is already a significant level of resources in schools, research has suggested that there is a paucity of ideas for their employment in all but the most mundane educational ways. Similar research also suggests that although many young people have access to sophisticated computer games technology within the home, they are rarely engaged in creative work or even have access to creative and artistic applications [2]. The opportunities that exist for photography and media work to step into this space may prove to be extremely productive. Two of the projects described here provide practical examples for teachers wanting to explore the concepts and practices related to new technologies, and their potential for educational and cultural work.

Young People, Education and Culture

Photography in education has tended to be at its strongest, where it exists at all, within the art departments of schools. One of the principal advantages of this has been the central importance placed on practical work in photography. However, it would be a mistake to believe that photography should be neatly slotted into art, as one of a range of media (this is the implication in the National Curriculum orders). Photography offers a challenge that goes to the core of the art curriculum and the philosophy that animates it.

Arts education at secondary level is beset by a contradiction. On the one hand formal education is the principal avenue through which young people experience a structured engagement with art and cultural activities, as participants. For the majority of young people, once they leave the education system their involvement in cultural activities declines significantly, except as consumers and audiences. On the other hand, secondary arts education often fails to recognise or engage with the rich potential of young people's cultural knowledge and creative abilities. This may be particularly evident in relation to the new cultural forms associated with computer technology. A recent report by the National Foundation for Educational Research comes to the disturbing conclusion, that for many young people the secondary arts curriculum and its delivery was considered a significant factor in turning them away from the arts [3].

Some commentators, notably Paul Willis, have responded by arguing that education is no longer a significant setting for young people's cultural activities, and that their creativity finds expression unproblematically in everyday life [4]. The evidence, however, suggests that Willis' populist line is at best optimistic. The school remains a place of central significance to most young people. The patterns of cultural activity and engagement established in education have lifelong implications. It is in this vein that the examples in this book have been developed, in the belief that education should foster an engagement with young people that both celebrates their identities and experiences, and opens up a space for the development of critical and reflective practices.

Photography in Education

Although any use of photography in schools could merit the title 'photography in education', the work described here has developed in a particular tradition, with its own guiding philosophy. At the heart of photography in education is the ambition to put in place a practical engagement between the structures of formal education and the cultural knowledge and experiences of young people. This gives the term its most specific definition.

It is also important to point out that photography in education work does not attempt to put in place any narrow technical definitions. The arguments originally put forward for the educational significance of photography centred on two features. First, photography is a medium with extremely diverse uses and connotations, ranging from art and science to popular culture and the family. Quite simply its impact on everyday life should not be ignored by educators. Second, photography is an extremely accessible medium, both in terms of cost and in its ease of use. Despite the over-technical nature of many specialist photographic courses, within primary and secondary education photography provides a medium with which young people can rapidly progress to a point where they are producing challenging and expressive work in a form that they understand and with which they are familiar. / *Conclusion*

It has been a central tenet of photography in education that classroom practice should relate to, and draw upon, the cultural activities and knowledge of young people. Part of the rationale for the inclusion of photographic work in formal educational settings was that it was able to achieve this more successfully than the cultural forms that were traditionally used in the art classroom. The Cultural Studies Department of the Cockpit Arts Workshop, who were active in the development of photography in education work from 1975 to 1988 say this: "We saw how it [photography] readily reached out beyond the school because in its popular forms it is used and consumed within everyday life" [5]. This remains an important reason for continuing to advocate photographic work in formal education.

Photography and New Technology

In recent years, as the technological base of photography has shifted from chemistry to electronics, and video and digital manipulation have become commonplace, so the need to expand the definition of the 'photographic' has become more pressing. Some have suggested that we are living in a post-photographic era. It is our belief that the continuing importance of photographic images to family life and the news media, for example, clearly contradicts such suggestions, and that the principal arguments for the inclusion of photography in a coherent way within the curriculum remain.

However, it is necessary to signal our intention to use the term photography in education in a broad sense in relation to technology. New developments in digital technology, and the greater availability of video, have served to extend the range of technologies which are available both in school and at home. The currency of these activities (alongside more traditional photography) with young people, and their ability to "reach out beyond school" provides a sound rationale for the kind of work illustrated here.

Background to the Manchester Photography Development Project

Although this is not the place to offer a detailed history of photography in education, and the important role that the Arts Council of England has played in the last twenty years, a few comments are needed to set this publication in context.

Since 1973, when it first recognised photography as a separate area of arts funding, the Arts Council of England has actively promoted the use of photography in schools. In its initial phase this involved the funding of photography residencies in schools, and support for educational work in galleries. The majority of the funding in this phase was provided for one-off initiatives.

Between 1983 and 1986 the Arts Council of England set about trying to create a more coherent and long-term strategy for the development of photography in formal education. As a result, during the period 1987 to 1994 six advisory posts were set up and run in collaboration with local education authorities across England. The aim was to create a network of photography specialists in several regions throughout the country, which could provide models of classroom practice and programmes of teacher training to local schools.

Although the advisory posts were broadly successful, providing a wealth of innovative and well documented examples, significant developments in the education system meant that this model of funding and collaboration was no longer viable. Changes to the management of schools resulting from the 1988 Education Reform Act, in particular the decline in influence of the Local Education Authorities, called for a new strategy to be adopted. The perspective shifted from the regional development of photography in education towards an attempt to influence national policy. This resulted in the setting up of a Photography and National Curriculum working party and subsequent submissions to the National Curriculum working groups for History, Geography and in particular Art (a submission was also made by the Photographers' Gallery to the History working group). This provided the basis for the publication in 1994 of *Creating Vision*, which provided an overarching argument for photography across the whole curriculum, and has been a touchstone for photography educators since.

In order to build on the success of *Creating Vision,* in 1994 the Arts Council of England set up three 3-year photography fellowships in collaboration with universities and independent photography organisations or galleries. One in Bristol, one in Middlesex, and this one in Manchester. The three way collaborations between schools, institutions of higher education and the photography sector promised to challenge the kinds of timid orthodoxies that the National Curriculum threatened to create, and ensure dissemination at a number of levels from classroom examples and exhibitions, to arguments at policy level and academic research papers.

The Four Case Studies

The four case studies offered here are all self-standing. Although they are presented in chronological order, readers should not feel bound by this sequence. We anticipate that teachers will be most interested in the examples that are closest to their own experience, and would encourage an interactive and intuitive use of the book, particularly in relation to classroom practice.

A particular feature shared by all the case studies is their dependence on collaborative partnerships. Artists, designers, photographers and external agencies such as museums and galleries can make a significant contribution to the development of the arts and media curriculum. Both teachers and students benefit from the stimulus provided by such collaborations, and the introduction to different ideas and ways of working that they provide. Although, to be successful, such projects require detailed planning and a greater level of commitment, often outside of normal teaching time, the rewards can be considerable, making connections between what happens in the classroom, the concerns of contemporary artistic and cultural practice, and the experiences of young people. Teachers developing similar projects on their own would perhaps require longer lead in times. We hope that the examples here provide an insight into some of the practical and logistical problems (and ways of overcoming them), as well as the educational benefits, and that others are encouraged to attempt similar projects.

Each of the case study examples engages with the educational issues I have outlined in this introduction in its own distinct way. It is not our intention to provide a 'how-to' book of photography in education, but rather to demonstrate through actual examples what is possible in real school contexts. It is hoped that this approach will inform and inspire teachers who share this commitment to photography in education, and persuade those who are new to the subject of its importance.

The first of the case studies (Grange High School) takes as its central theme the question of identity. What is it that makes us who we are? Is identity a single unified thing, always constant, or does it seem to change constantly, eluding our grasp? How can we represent it? During the 1980's much of contemporary artistic and photographic practice was concerned with the idea of cultural identity and the exploration of cultural difference. The work of the British Asian artist Sutapa Biswas was used to introduce students to the idea of representing their own identities through photography. The students were also encouraged to collect and make use of their own image bank of family photographs and found images (photography work does not always have to involve expensive cameras). This approach enabled a genuine integration of critical and practical studies, and extended the conventional limits of the art curriculum. The examples of student work reproduced here along with the students' own comments suggest a complex investigation of the idea of identity and its representation in a visual form. The project also provided the basis for later work at the school in the area of personal and social education (PSE).

The second case study (Ellen Wilkinson High School) asked the students to explore their own environment and the relationship between past, present and future. The theme of 'Time Capsule 2045' meant students had to devise ways of representing their world to those to whom it would be unfamiliar. This project also explored a range of technologies from conventional chemical photography to video and digital imaging. The outcomes of the project formed the basis for a web site on the Internet.

The third case study (Queen Elizabeth High School) again takes up the idea of representing the students' own environment – in this case the town of Middleton near the school on the Langley housing estate in Greater Manchester. In this example, instead of trying to create a record of the place and what it means to live there, the students were attempting to simulate the real experience of being in Middleton through a virtual reality video performance. This project is the odd one out of the four in that it takes place in the context of a media studies syllabus, whereas the others are all based in art departments. In this respect it serves as an illustration of the value of practical work in media studies, and the common ground that photographic media can open up between the two.

The final case study (St. Paul's High School) uses the landscape work of the artist Kate Mellor as a starting point for the students' own explorations of the interrelationship between local environment and identity. The students from Wythenshawe in Greater Manchester used conventional black and white and colour photography in the context of an endorsed photography syllabus. The work they produced demonstrates that the power of 'straight' photography as a means of representation is not diminished, even in the era of the digital camera and the Internet.

Photography has always depended to a greater extent than more established subjects on the enthusiasm and commitment of particular individuals. In the final section of the book Jane Brake reflects on her experiences over the last three years, organising, arguing for, and delivering photography in education. Her arguments concerning the future development of photography in the curriculum are worthy of our considered attention.

The outcomes of the four projects, alongside the comments and responses from the teachers, students and artists involved, bear testimony to the benefits photography in education work has given to these individuals and schools. By sharing the examples in this publication we hope many others can benefit from similar initiatives in the future.

Darren Newbury

Notes

[1] Isherwood, S., & Stanley, N. (eds.) (1994) Creating Vision: Photography and the National Curriculum. Manchester: Cornerhouse Publications.

[2] See Buckingham, D., & Sefton-Green, J. (1996) Digital Visions: New Opportunities for Multimedia Learning: Project Report. London, Institute of Education; and Whittaker, R. (1995) Adult-Free Zones: Children and Entertainment Technology. 20:20, No.3, pp35-37.

[3] Harland, J., Kinder, K., & Hartley, K. (1995) Arts in Their View: A study of youth participation in the arts. Slough: National Foundation for Educational Research.

[4] Willis, P. (1990) Common Culture: Symbolic Work at Play in the Everyday Cultures of the Young. Buckingham: Open University Press.

[5] Cultural Studies Department, Cockpit Arts Workshop (1985) Using Photography in Schools: A Cultural Studies Approach. London: Cockpit.

Here and Now

Grange High School

Artist: Sutapa Biswas

"Memories are strange things. Like a ghost, sensed but never seen, the past haunts our present. We seize memories and grasp at vague recollections, impelled by our desire to map the journey which has brought us to here and now."

Gilane Tawadros

Students: Mahmod Ali, Jessica Begum, Rakha Begum, Maria Bell, Vikkie Charnock, Anamul Hoque, Zahieda Khanom, Monixa Mistry, Habiba Mosammat.

This section is a revised version of the article 'Photography in Education - The Grange School Project' by Jane Brake, Patricia Procter and Keith Walker, first published in the *Journal of Art and Design Education*, Volume 15 Number 1.

Grange is an 11-16 multi-cultural school situated in the centre of Oldham in Greater Manchester. The majority of the students are children or grandchildren of migrant workers who came from Bangladesh, India and Pakistan, initially to work in the textile factories and related industries. Many of the students at Grange have been affected by migration or displacement in some way or another.

The school has a flourishing art department with committed staff and good facilities. The windows of the art department overlook a jumbled cityscape of industrial architecture, mill chimneys and red brick housing, spreading out towards the city of Manchester. Students regularly eat their lunch in the art rooms and continue their artwork after school is finished. Thus the art department functions as a social space, where students attend voluntarily, and provides continuity in the hectic school day during which students move from room to room.

Project Summary

School: Grange High School
Teacher: Barbara Padgett
Curriculum: GCSE Art &
Design (unendorsed)
Students: Year 11
Artist: Sutapa Biswas
Partners: Oldham Art Gallery
and Manchester
Metropolitan University
Duration: one term

At Key Stage 4 students take a GCSE unendorsed syllabus and are able to explore a range of disciplines, including painting and drawing, textiles and ceramics. Prior to this project the department had done little practical photographic work, though photographic images were used regularly as a primary source in painting and drawing, where all students complete a self-portrait drawn from a photograph taken by the teacher.

The head of art, Barbara Padgett, approached the photography in education worker at Manchester Metropolitan University in the summer term of 1994 requesting help to develop photographic work in the school, and enable students to gain practical experience of working with photography. The suggestion was attractive for several reasons. It provided an opportunity to develop photographic work within the context of GCSE practice. This was an area of particular interest because any long term development of photography education in schools needs to address the question of examinations and assessment. It also allowed for an integrated approach to practical and critical studies, with the exhibition at Oldham Art Gallery by the artist Sutapa Biswas providing a focus for the subsequent project and an inspiration for the students' own work. Finally, given that the department had little experience of photography they were particularly receptive to new ideas and ways of working.

The initial discussions led to a project on the theme of 'Identity' which took place at the school in the Autumn of 1994 with a group of ten year 11 students. The members of the group were a representative sample selected by their teachers.

The Project

The aim of the project was to start from the students' experiences, as a way of engaging them in an exploration of visual culture, and enabling them to develop an individual sense of purpose in relation to their own work. In choosing the theme 'Identity' it was assumed that each student would be able to engage with the theme in some way, drawing on personal experience, social or political awareness of identity. This approach also served as an introduction to contemporary artistic practice, where during the 1980's issue-based work displaced the predominant modernist concern with formalism and abstraction. The following aspects of the project were given particular emphasis:

Jessica Begum

- to enhance the art and design syllabus by providing a photography option within the unendorsed course.

- to establish a model of practice for photography in secondary art and design education.

- to develop the potential of previous work on identity, linking with the students' previous project in drawing and painting, and allowing scope for in depth exploration of the theme.

- to provide a focus for effective engagement with 'Synapse', an exhibition of work by Sutapa Biswas which was part of the Signals Women's Photography Festival at Oldham Art Gallery during September and October of 1994 (the students also had an opportunity to meet and talk to the artist).

- to encourage consideration of content as well as technical and formal concerns, and promote individual interpretations and personal lines of enquiry.

- to explore the potential for collaborative practice between artists, teachers, gallery education staff and students.

The scheme of work devised for the project comprised three stages.

stage one

Students were introduced to the theme and prepared for the gallery visits. They were told that they would need to develop visual resources relevant to the theme and that this material would be utilised in a gallery-based workshop. During the three week period of preparation each student created their own personal image bank on colour slide film. A wide range of personally significant items and mementoes were photographed as well as aspects of the local environment. These collected images proved to be an important part of the students later practical work.

The students were also given the opportunity to discuss examples of Sutapa's earlier work which related to their own on the theme of self-portraiture. It was anticipated that preparing students in this way would enable them to gain more from the gallery visits and subsequent school-based work.

stage two

The students visited the exhibition, explored its contents and participated in a related workshop jointly run by Jane Brake and the gallery's photography officer. The students' own photographic images, produced in the preceding three weeks, were discussed in order to identify why some were more successful than others, and to consider the means by which the images were 'read'. Following an editing exercise, particular images were selected and projected directly onto the students' faces, clothing and hands with the outcomes being re-photographed by the photography officer.

This approach mirrored that used by Sutapa in the exhibition 'Synapse', where she re-photographed images projected onto her stomach. This idea of projection onto the body was borrowed to allow students to engage with a simple process of mapping visual references to their external existence onto their bodies in order to help them find a language with which to speak about identity. In a subsequent visit to the gallery students met with Sutapa and heard her talk about the relationship between her personal history, cultural influences and the content of her work.

stage three

The final phase was school-based. It was designed to encourage students to develop personal lines of enquiry on the theme of identity through to the completion of practical work. They were initially introduced to basic black and white processing and printing skills, and eventually to studio work, creative darkroom techniques and montage. Integral to the progress of the scheme was the continuing consideration of works by other artists who have similarly explored the theme of identity. Students were given further supporting visual and written material on the theme.

Identity
finger prints, blood, DNA
identity card, passport, photofit
race, class, gender,
sexuality, disability
nationality, heritage, roots
personality, pyschology,
essence, childhood,
family, memory
job, status experience,
environment, feelings, thoughts,
dreams, desires place, belonging
what makes you the same?
what makes you different?
what makes you you?

From student handout

An intriguing element of the project was the way in which the sketchbook came to be used. Jane Brake's sketchbook was originally presented as a concrete example of an ideas book, in order to encourage students to experiment with similar working processes. However, its function was extended as Jane started to compile pages on which were written her thoughts regarding the development of each student's thinking and ideas. A number of students on their own initiative replied to these notes by adding written responses to the questions that had been raised. In consequence, a dialogue developed which was to inform and influence the students' structuring, content and presentation of their own journals.

Four Students

In considering the impact of the project and evaluating its successes, we have decided to present the work of four students alongside both their own and Jane's commentary. Each of the three elements gives a slightly different perspective on the students' engagement with the project. It is hoped that this approach will give an insight into its complexity.

Maria Bell

Identity covers many things about people and their environment. An identity separates people and personality to make them into an individual, no-one and nothing is exactly identical. With this in mind I decided I would interpret the theme of identity by basing my work on what makes us what we are. For example our parents talk to us and influence our personality, like the media, teachers and what we see and hear in our everyday life.

When I was designing my work I was introduced to Sutapa Biswas, a photographic artist, who I met at Oldham Art Gallery. Her actual work didn't influence me, but the way her work was presented gave me an insight into what my final design could look like. A particular piece gave me an idea which could involve the photographs with the text whilst exaggerating the idea of the media influences on our personality.

I've done more research than I've ever done before...in my sketchbooks I'd just practice drawing at home or designing a ceramic piece, but now I've got photocopies, other people's work, notes, and I've developed my ideas more, that's why I keep jumping from idea to idea.

Maria Bell

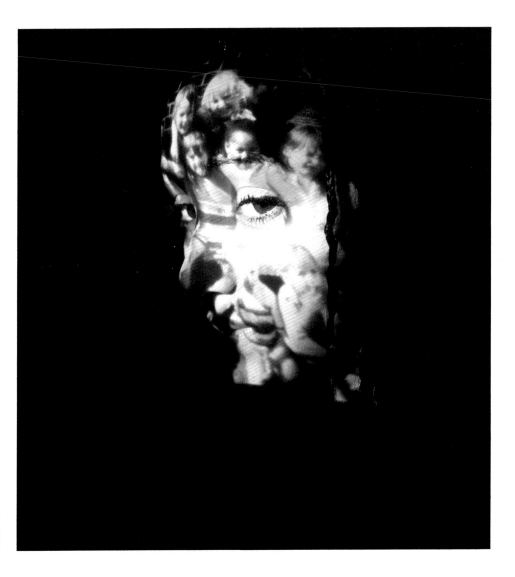

Maria Bell

Maria had collected small objects of personal significance and family photographs from her childhood. In preparation for the gallery workshop she had produced a sketch of her idea, which involved projecting a photograph of herself as a child onto her eye, in order to represent her view of her position within a close knit family. She soon became aware that it was not possible, for technical reasons, to realise her idea as originally conceived. She decided instead to use a photograph of herself as a young girl, the only black child amongst a group of white friends, and to use her entire face as a backdrop. The image she created is stunning, but also disturbing. Her face glows against the density of the background. The projected image is masked within the crescent shape of her face, and her eyes, throwing a slightly hooded, sidelong glance, create the focal point.

Maria also produced a second image by projecting another photograph of herself as a child into a blue trinket box held in her two hands against her blue jumper. Unlike the first picture, the child's eyes look directly into the camera. The blueness of the box is echoed in the background and contrasts with the skin tone of her hands. The reduced colour scheme helps to focus the mind on the meaning she is intending to convey. The image speaks of the secret thoughts of the child, the way in which childhood becomes part of adult identity, as if we carry it around with us in a box, intact.

Maria thought deeply about identity, what precisely she wanted to say in each image and how best to convey this. She found it hard to relinquish her first idea, seeing it as a compromise of her original intentions. Because of the depth of her feelings she found the spontaneous approach during the gallery workshop difficult. She was, however, reassured when the photographs were developed.

Maria Bell

Maria's work in the school-based phase of the project took up the theme of childhood in a more general way than she had initially planned. She decided not to concentrate specifically on herself and her family because she did not want, at this stage, to deal with some of the complex issues of race involved in her own life. She created a montage using a number of different elements: black and white photographs of herself, images from magazines and newspapers, and a mask of her face created in ceramics. The words 'Determine Identity' help to link these elements into a whole which presents a view of how identity is constructed.

From the outset Maria set high standards for herself and worked with determination to realise her ambitions. The effect of her involvement could be clearly discerned in a later project. In returning to the theme of self-portraiture, but this time explored through the medium of ceramics, she incorporated found materials making explicit reference to her montage. The project had the effect of expanding her visual vocabulary, and giving a greater degree of purpose to her art making activities.

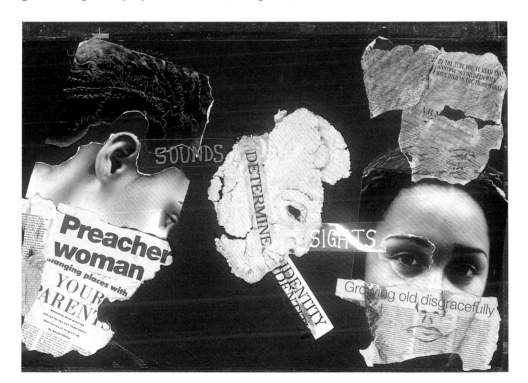

Maria Bell

process and on the formal elements. The students worked with darkroom techniques such as solarisation and multiple printing, using each other as models and also featuring a range of recurring motifs from the local environment such as grave stones, swings or industrial architecture. A project that was able to build on these strengths, but which opened onto new areas seemed appropriate. Initial thoughts suggested it would be interesting to give the students a chance to try using colour photography or digital imaging for instance, and to do something which could be seen in a context outside the school.

Adele Dunne
Aimee Goodwin
Justina Potter
Claire Scott

Phil Verral contacted Jane some time after her initial visit. The possibility of a residency was discussed and Jane felt that it may be possible to secure funding from the Arts Council of England for the Time Capsule idea. The project was given a further impetus by a favourable Ofsted report. The report raised an interesting point about the benefits of more collaboration between technology and art, and as a result Phil Verral was appointed Head of Art and Technology (he was previously Head of Art). It also confirmed and supported the decision to work with digital technology on the project. A funding application for the project was submitted in February '95.

The success of the application meant that the project was given the go-ahead. It was decided that the appointment of an artist in residence would be advertised nationally, as well as a mail shot to local organisations and individuals in the area with a track record in this kind of work. Chris Dooks from Cleveland was appointed. He showed some stunning video work at the interview, and impressed the interview panel by producing a sketch book in which he had already started to work up ideas for the project. It was however agreed at the interview that he was inexperienced, and although he had worked on a number of projects and directed his own films he had never taken on a project of this size. It was decided to appoint him, but acknowledged that he would 'need support'.

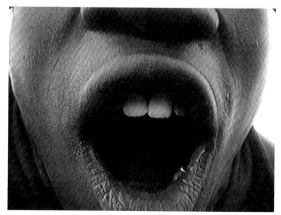

Gary Barnes

Simeon Small

Project Theme

The theme for the project was the idea of producing time capsules for the year 2045. It was envisaged that this would enable the students to explore questions of personal and group identity, memory and environment. It was intended to provide a forum in which students' voices could be heard - to enable them to take their own lives and ideas about their future as subject matter, and encourage them to think specifically about how their images might communicate with a wider audience. The theme also provided an umbrella unifying the diversity of media - sound, text, moving and still images - that students were expected to experience during the project.

Project Aims

The project had the following general aims:

- to explore the potential of multimedia work in the art curriculum.

- to emphasise multicultural and critical studies elements of the curriculum by engaging in issue-based practice as part of a GCSE Art and Design (endorsed photography) course.

- to use photography to stimulate cross-curricular practice.

- to work on the theme of identity and memory to produce time capsules for the year 2045.

- to enable students to engage with a wide audience through public dissemination of their work.

In addition to these aims it was hoped that the project would have a longer term impact. Within the school the intention was that staff would: (i) become aware of the potential for using new technologies such as digital imaging as part of ongoing curriculum work; (ii) begin to develop the skills and knowledge to achieve this; and (iii) develop partnerships for future collaboration on educational multimedia projects. Beyond the school context, and particularly through the communication potential of the web site, the project was intended as an exemplar, and a point of reference for similar projects in a national and international context (the school had already established links with a school in Japan through its Internet access).

Scheme of Work

Work started in September 1995 and was scheduled to run for approximately 10 weeks during the autumn term, with some residency hours reserved for the following term. During the first few weeks of the project Jane Brake also acted as facilitator, booking equipment, transporting equipment and making sure all the financial things were in place.

Project Summary

School: Queen Elizabeth High School
Teacher: Graham Smith
Curriculum: GCSE Media Studies
Students: year 10
Artist: Anton Hecht
Partners: Viewpoint Photography
Gallery and Manchester
Metropolitan University
Duration: one term

As with all the projects described in this book, Video Reality involved collaboration between a number of partners. In this case it was a three-way collaboration between Jane Brake the photography in education worker at Manchester Metropolitan University, the school and Viewpoint Photography Gallery in Salford. The initial idea for the project came from the artist Anton Hecht who sent a proposal to Viewpoint. The Video Reality idea had been developed by Anton in his own work, and had already proved a successful basis for educational work during a three month residency at schools in Cheshire.

The School Context

The school provided an exciting context in which to place the project for a number of reasons. It was an ideal opportunity to deepen and extend the institutional links that already existed, and to develop expertise in the school across subject boundaries. At the invitation of the Head of Art, Celia Davies, Jane had worked in the school previously doing photography with year 9 students. Celia had also attended a short course on photography in education at the university. The previous commitment to photography work and the understanding of the issues involved ensured support for the project, which was perceived as offering considerable benefit to teaching in the school, as well as an exciting opportunity for its students. The school also had a purpose built media room and edit suite of which the project would be able to make full use.

The Curriculum Context

Media studies was part of the school's Expressive Arts department, which also included Music, Drama, Art and Dance. This context is perhaps somewhat unusual in that media studies has generally had its strongest links with English. Nevertheless, this suggested that the practical elements (visual and sound) of video production would be well supported. Given the tendency in some media studies teaching to emphasise conceptual and written learning outcomes above the practical, this may even be considered to be of benefit to the project and potentially instructive for media teaching generally. The project had the potential to dissolve some of the artificial boundaries between practical and theoretical work that affect photography in education, as it is placed alternately in art and in media as part of English.

The teacher and curriculum development aspects of the project were particularly prominent as this was the first year media studies had been offered as an examination subject at the school, and the teacher, Graham Smith, was not a media specialist and had no previous formal training in the subject. Graham's account of his introduction to the subject is perhaps not untypical of the haphazard way in which photography and media work has tended to develop in formal education, and provides an interesting insight into the long-term value of this project:

It goes back about five or six years, when in those days I was the youngest member of staff and every school in Rochdale was given a video camera by the authority, and no-one in our school really knew what to do with it and I was the youngest member of staff and therefore I must be into technological things so it landed on my doorstep. I used it first as part of my GCSE music work. When we introduced expressive arts, there seemed a natural way there, because for expressive arts you needed to have two different art forms so I could teach music and media or video work together. So that's how I started this year. September we actually started a media studies GCSE, so really I was just thrown in at the deep end.

The Project Brief

Although no written brief was handed out to the students, they were told that they were going to produce a video about Middleton - the nearest town to Langley and where most Langley residents go to do their shopping. The central idea of the project was that the video would provide the centrepiece of a virtual reality performance. The video would be played through the camera viewed close to one eye (as if it were a virtual reality headset). By wearing an eye patch on the other eye individual audience members would participate in the 'virtual' experience of being in Middleton. The action would be linked to the participant by the constant presence in the frame of the hand of the camera operator.

Whilst the video was being viewed, the students would lead the participants round and present them with a range of tactile surfaces, arranged on a staff, which related to the

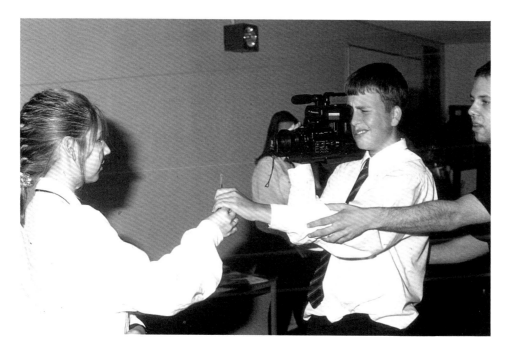

Pupils working in the classroom

action of the video. The intention was that this would provide participants with an interactive experience.

Two aspects of the brief are particularly important to the overall intentions of the project. First, the students were being asked to document and explore an environment familiar to them. The approach presented the opportunity for the students to examine their own experience from a new perspective, and to share their vision with a real audience. It positioned them as investigators and commentators on their own social environment, speaking for themselves rather than being spoken to or about. Second, the project sought to explore issues surrounding new technology, in particular their potential for creating simulated realities. This is an area of considerable current interest in cultural and educational debates generally; it also had the potential to tap into the cultural activities that the students engaged in outside of formal education, for example the use of virtual reality computer games.

The Project Schedule

Anton Hecht worked with the media studies group and their teacher, Graham Smith, one session a week (two hours) for the duration of the term. The project was scheduled in three stages: introduction and planning; production; editing and preparation of the performance.

Introduction and planning

The first phase of the project introduced the students to the technical and conceptual aspects of the project. Early sessions were spent introducing the project, getting used to the camera and talking about scripting. Alongside this Anton introduced a number of words and concepts that were new to the students (and to the teacher). On the whole the students responded well to the challenge and enjoyed learning this new vocabulary, words such as 'intertextuality' and 'postmodernism'. Anton adopted a very free flowing style in these sessions, with informal discusssions tending to continue beyond the end of the lesson. A disadvantage of this was that it reduced time for practical work, which some students were eager to begin.

"The planning was very boring and I couldn't wait to go out and film"

Production

The students were divided into two groups for the production stage. This consisted of a trip to Middleton where the video shots were filmed. Several students also did sound recordings, interviewing shoppers about their views on Middleton.

Editing and Preparation of the Performance

The following weeks were spent editing the material, practising the performance and then making any necessary adjustments to the edited material. The students practised

the finished piece with other students in the school in preparation for the performance at Viewpoint Photography Gallery. The performance took place on Sunday 17th December, when a small audience of parents and gallery visitors were led through the video reality experience by a group of students.

Issues and Outcomes

Following the completion of the project, the participants were asked to reflect on its strengths and weaknesses, what they enjoyed and what they did not, and any implications that flowed from the project. The media teacher, the artist and two students were interviewed on tape. The students had earlier in the programme been asked to complete an evaluation questionnaire about the project and its relationship to their use of media outside of the school environment. The evaluation process highlighted a number of issues and outcomes that are worthy of further consideration.

Curriculum Development

The project provided an interesting model for curriculum development. Photography and associated media forms such as video play a central part in young people's cultural activities outside of formal education. Yet photography and media studies teachers have had to struggle to retain the position of their subjects in the curriculum without the kind of formal support provided for mainstream subjects. Many of the teachers who introduce media and photography examinations to their school do so with little more than their own enthusiasm and commitment to sustain them. There has traditionally been little in the way of training and curriculum support to guide teachers in their development of such work. This increases the importance and value of the alternative kinds of curriculum support provided through a project such as this one.

The teacher on this project clearly valued the input made available by this project. It offered not just a one-off experience, but also a means of sustaining and developing the work he had initiated:

"I haven't ever had any training, which is why the experience with Anton coming in has been brilliant. It has really been training in school, as we've been going along. And learning not just from the project that we've done but other lessons that Anton has taken. The things he has been talking about with one group, I have used with another group, and I shall write up and that shall be my scheme of work for this term"

Further comments from the teacher indicate that it would have been of considerable value to separate those aspects of the project that contributed to his own development as a teacher of media studies, from the actual delivery of the project itself:

*SEE TEACHER'S SCHEME OF WORK
AT THE END OF THIS SECTION*

"I feel I have been one of the students in many of the lessons because of my lack of knowledge about some of the things Anton has been doing. I have definitely learned things in each lesson. Now my decision has either been do I stand at the front with Anton and hold his hand or, what I have actually done most of the time is sit at the back and be a student and allowed Anton most of the time just to deliver."

Discussion also revealed the way in which the project allowed normal teaching and preparation constraints to be loosened somewhat. This was something the teacher, and the students, clearly found exciting:

"I gave Anton the requirements for the syllabus for the practical section and we just thrashed through, and I think it was trying to bend what we were going to do into the syllabus, as opposed to the normal way we work it: there's the syllabus and we think of things that fit together"

"One of the problems is that I wouldn't be allowed to function that way. The way things are going, less and less have you got that kind of freedom, unless you pull people in like Anton."

" I would have liked, perhaps it is just the teacher in me, I would have liked a plan for the whole of the ten weeks and I would have liked to have known from week to week what we were going to be doing. I think Anton shoots from the hip really...It works brilliantly."

Teaching Cultural Practice

Media affects my life probably more than anything else, as it is entertainment as well as the only awareness of things which go on in this country and abroad. I spend most of my time being entertained by the media. If there was no media everybody would be bored with hardly anything to talk about.

The words of this student, taken from his project evaluation, capture succinctly the social, cultural, educational and political importance of media forms for the lives of many young people in contemporary western societies. It would be hard to imagine life without television, video, film, photography or newspapers; as this student so astutely observes, our use of the media is for many of us so integrated with daily life that without them we would be literally lost for words.

This student's statement also tells us something else about the relationship of young people to contemporary media. They are entertained by them, educated and informed by them, but rarely are they able to exercise control over them. This is not to suggest that young people, or anyone for that matter, uncritically absorb the messages that are directed at them (this student in his evaluation was able to recognise his own critical reading abilities), but simply to argue that access to practical photographic media for creative and communicative purposes is of considerable educational and cultural value. The opportunities offered for such engagement are insufficient. Video Reality positioned the students as creators and communicators in their own right, with something of significance to say about their own lives and experiences.

It has been a weakness of some examples of media studies teaching that they have place greatest emphasis on written work as a means of assessing educational outcomes. Practical media work has been reduced to repetitive simulations of existing forms, or exercises with the express aim of demonstrating theoretical understanding. Such approaches often fail to hold any real value for students. This project demonstrates the value of an alternative and more engaging model of practical media studies work. Students were not only encouraged to take control of their own learning, but also to make their own environment the centre of the project. This gave a sense of purpose to the students' work, and increased their confidence in their own ideas and abilities:

" I learnt that you don't just have to watch a video you can get involved"

"I didn't do anything other than purely supervise them. They decided what they were going to film, how they were going to film it. It has given them a kind of independence, maybe an independence which they don't get in other subjects, where they are definitely sat down and they are given instructions or given exercises to do. This has given them a kind of independence and they are able to, I suppose, be responsible for their own learning is the educational jargon for it."

The approach weakened boundaries between the theoretical and practical aspects of media production. The project could have worked equally well in the context of the art curriculum, and in fact gave the opportunity for students to share in the status of being an artist.

"Having a video camera tends to affect people..you somehow become something other than yourself..an artist...control over the content actually makes them into artists"

The context of media studies within an expressive arts department gave a valuable extra dimension to the project, allowing it to develop without having to worry too much about the constraints imposed by rigid subject boundaries:

"I think the children's perception of media, or why they perhaps chose media was because they thought it was video cameras, and it was playing around with video cameras, making films which people then sit down and watch. Now I think with the work that Anton has been doing with them they have seen a different way to it. Art for them is painting and drawing, and now they are producing something which we are calling art and they are seeing examples of work like this. I think it has been a real eye-opener for them."

The Process of Making

"With this piece of work the process of making it is a very social thing, round the leisure centre, round the shopping centre, introducing themselves to people and things like that, and so they got something out of that process, and I got something out of watching them, that is something I never really considered as part of the project before."   Anton Hecht

Anton's reflections on the process of making that the project involved makes a very interesting point. We tend to think of media production in technical terms - this is often over-represented in the way photography and video are taught. Yet, making a video is also very much a social process. This applies to the interaction that goes on within the production team, as well as to the interaction between producers and subjects. In the evaluation of the project, this experience came through strongly from the students:

"I enjoyed going to Middleton and meeting people to do the interviewing."

"I most enjoyed going into Middleton and filming meeting people and seeing their reactions to us video filming them."

The project's emphasis on group work was very well received by the students, most of whom said that they valued the discussion it provoked, and the continual interchange of ideas helped their own individual development:

"I find working in a group is great because you can get different ideas and opinions of what they want to do and you can compare your own ideas too."

It is perhaps unsurprising that some gender differences were evident in the way in which individual students engaged with the project. The girls tended to place greater emphasis on the discussion aspects and the social dimension of meeting people whilst producing the video. The boys on the other hand tended to respond more enthusiastically to the technical and performance aspects of the project:

"I enjoyed the actual filming most because it was fun and enjoyable actually working with the cameras."

Conclusion

The project facilitated and extended the process of curriculum development that Graham Smith had initiated at the school. The collaborative partnership involved in the project made available expertise and a perspective on educational practice that could not have happened otherwise. The project provided a genuine learning experience for all those involved. More importantly perhaps, this example has something to contribute to the development of media education in the wider context. It provides an innovative example of practical media work. It also makes the argument for a greater integration of analytical media and practical arts approaches to cultural work in the curriculum. Although the text in this chapter, and rightly so, has concentrated on the educational issues and outcomes of the project this is only half the story. The video work shown here is not merely an illustration of the educational approach, but stands as an integral piece of visual culture. Although the still images cannot recapture all the qualities of the video, nor the excitement of the performance at the Gallery, it does give an indication of the achievement. We leave knowing more about the students' world and how they see it.

Teacher's Scheme of Working

The following is the scheme of work devised by the media teacher Graham Smith as a result of his experience working with Anton on the Video Reality project. It presumes students will have completed two earlier schemes on basic camera skills and understanding media language.

Video Reality Project

AIMS: students will begin to develop the necessary skills to produce a five minute video reality product. This will be a guide around the students' community. The audience will watch the video through the viewfinder of the video camera and touch the objects seen on a sensory staff, thus giving the reality illusion.

OBJECTS AND ASSESSMENT: By the end of this project each student should, according to their abilities and with varying degrees of success, be able to:

1. Use a video camera, developing their skills.

2. Use an editing suite to perform simple editing tasks, including adding a soundtrack.

3. Plan and then shoot, following a storyboard.

Stage One: Dummy Run

STIMULUS: a) introduce the topic, explaining the processes involved in making a video reality product. Firstly around school (as a dummy run) and then the main project, in our community. b) review basic camera shots learnt previously (eg long shot, close-up)
ACTIVITY: c) class discussion of possible locations in school that could be used and the tactile sensations that you might experience (eg keyboard in music, ball in games, paint brush in art). d) divide into groups of four. Each group to film at four different locations, editing to be done in camera.
Evaluation: e) groups review their own work.

Stage Two: Planning

STIMULUS: a) whole class discussion on successes and failures of dummy run. b) explain the concept of the storyboard. c) introduce the idea of producing a video reality guide to Middleton.

ACTIVITY: d) in groups list interesting/unusual locations in the community and discuss tactile sensations you might expect to come across. e) groups select a maximum of ten locations and produce a storyboard. f) plan the order of the shoot and make any prior contacts necessary.

EVALAUATION: g) group assessment of others storyboards.

Stage Three: The Shoot

STIMULUS: a) in the time available groups must acquire all necessary shots.

ACTIVITY: b) in groups, shoot according to the planned order.

EVALAUATION: c) watch in camera scenes shoot, and re-shoot as necessary. d) whole class discussion on the experience of the shoot and the work of other groups.

Stage Four: Editing

STIMULUS: a) teacher input on basic editing techniques (eg. cross fade, clean cut).

ACTIVITY: b) students use storyboard to check all scenes have been filmed - some reviews may be necessary. c) students edit down.

EVALAUATION: group and/or class discussion of edited film.

Stage Five: Soundtrack

STIMULUS: a) discuss role of music in film and television - watching examples.

ACTIVITY: b) in groups discuss.plan their soundtrack. c) record soundtrack onto edited video tape.

EVALAUATION: group and/or class discussion of edited film with soundtrack.

Stage Six: Sensory staff

STIMULUS: a) explain the role of the sensory staff.

ACTIVITY: b) students in their original groups discuss tactile sensations required and how that sensation can be reproduced. c) students design and make sensory staffs.

EVALUATION: c) groups try out their videos with sensory staffs on other groups. d) whole class discussion on successfulness of sensory staffs.

Stage Seven: Rehearsal

STIMULUS: a) explain the role of 'audience questionnaire' in the evaluation of the project.

ACTIVITY: b) whole class devise questionnaire. c) students rehearse the 'performance' of the video, with students outside of the media group. There is a need for students to experience different roles - guides and prompt.

EVALAUATION: d) whole class discussion of the rehearsal.

Stage Eight: Performance

STIMULUS: a) THIS IS IT!

ACTIVITY: b) public performance

EVALAUATION: c) audience questionnaires and verbal feedback. d) students write their own personal evaluation of the project.

Stages 4, 5 and 6 may need to be done in rotation depending on equipment and facilities available. Each stage is approximately equal to three 50 minute sessions.

RESOURCES: Video cameras (1 per group), video tapes (for recording and editing), TV monitors, video players, storyboard sheets, CD player, cassette player, examples of music from films/television, broom handles and material as necessary for sensory staffs.

ASSESSMENT: 1 Completed video - teacher assessment; 2. Questionnaires completed by audience; 3. Students own accounts and written evaluations.

KEY TERMS: Video reality, storyboard, editing/camera shots and their specific terminology, sensory.

DIFFERENTIATION: By outcome and by support.

TEACHING AND LEARNING STYLES: Teacher led, small group work, whole class work and experiential learning.

EQUAL OPPOTUNITIES: Same task for all students.

CROSS-CURRICULAR: Technology (design and making of sensory staffs); Music (role of music in film/television); English (devising a questionnaire); Art (looking at contemporary practice, making and analysing visual imagery).

Our Wythenshawe

St. Paul's High School

Students: Danielle Austin, Julie Bould, Alison Buckley, Leanne Crump, Angela Holt, Sarah Hyland, Sarah Lynch, Christopher Lynes, Anthony Nolan, Martin Thorpe, Laura Wilcox.

Our Wythenshawe took place during the summer term of 1996 with a group of 10 year ten students on a GCSE Art and Design (endorsed photography) course at St.Paul's High School in Greater Manchester. The students used an exhibition of landscape photographs by Kate Mellor at Viewpoint Photography Gallery as a starting point for their own investigation of the relationship between identity and place. The exhibition, entitled 'Island: The Sea Front', was the result of a three and a half year long project. Using a panoramic camera, the photographer travelled around the perimeter of Britain photographing and recording her impressions of what she saw. Kate describes her approach:

"I wanted to use an essentially British posture, an inherited system which ordered the land, precise and mathematical, which told you where you were and where your standpoint lay, which resulted in pre-measured points - the grid reference system. So, beginning with Shakespeare Cliff, Dover being a traditional exit-entry port, I went to record the view, with these pre-set standards and a compass, looking at the horizon from where particular grid lines crossed the coast, a piece of work shaped by the land out of which it rose."

The work is a richly detailed exploration of the relationship between geographical place, nationality and identity.

Project Theme

Although, it is clear that the school project could not achieve the scope and depth of Kate's work, the broad thematic approach was expected to provide a fruitful starting point for the GCSE students. In addition, it was felt that there was considerable value for the students in meeting and talking with the photographer and understanding the way in which she worked. The focus for the practical work was the students' local environment - how it was experienced and what meanings it held. The students were encouraged to use the project as an opportunity to explore their own understanding of the area in which they lived, and to develop a personal response within the context of the broader theme.

Project Summary

School: St Paul's High School
Teacher: Mr Addis
Curriculum: GCSE Art & Design
(endorsed photography)
Students: year 10
Artist: Kate Mellor
Partners: Viewpoint Photography
Gallery and Manchester
Metropolitan University
Duration: one term

Schedule

Due to work experience and two school trips planned for the summer term the project had to be scheduled over eight weeks.

week 1

Introduction to the project.

Slide show and discussion of landscape photography.

Exercise in image analysis using a photograph from Kate Mellor's exhibition.

week 2

Mapping Our School.

Exercise and presentation of 3 minute slide tape shows.

week 3

Visit to Viewpoint Photography Gallery to meet Kate Mellor and see her exhibition.

weeks 4 & 5

Developing films and printing material generated in their own time.

weeks 6, 7 & 8

Split into two groups one group going out with Jane Brake for the first half of the lesson, whilst the other group printed and developed new films. Activities rotated for the second half of the lesson. The brief for the field trips was Boundary and Interior.

Obviously the tight schedule placed limitations on the work that could be attempted. However, in order that the students can achieve a good standard of photography, and that the exploratory aspects of the project can be seen through to finished photographic work, a number of additional sessions took place during the Autumn term.

The project schedule was constructed around three key activities:

- engagement with the photographic work of a practising artist

- introductory exercise of mapping the school

- extended photographic field work

The first two activities had particular learning objectives: the introduction of students to ways of analysing and thinking about photographic imagery; and the introduction to a theme-centred approach to photographic practice. The extended photographic work was intended to give the students an opportunity to use and develop what they had learned in a context which allowed them to explore issues that had personal importance - their experience of where they lived.

A Note on Working Processes

It was important in this project, as in all the others, that emphasis was placed on the process of the project as well as the final products. The students were therefore introduced to the use of a sketch book or ideas book at the beginning of the project, and encouraged to explore its use in relation to their practical and theoretical work. It was emphasised that the students need not be particularly precious about what they included, and that a sketch book could be a collection of rough ideas and a place of experimentation rather than a finished piece of work. Their initial fears about the purpose of the sketch book (being purely for drawing) were alleviated. Students were given a handout which included a list of suggestions as to possible material they might want to include:

- writing: diary or log book, technical notes about photographs, quotations, songs, rhymes, stories: these could be from friends or family, a book you are reading, newspaper or tv programme. Don't worry about spelling in your sketchbook, it is your ideas that are important.

- sketches: photographers can use sketches to help with composition, it doesn't matter if you think you can't draw, as long as you record the basic idea. You can use spoilt prints or contact sheets cut up as sketches. Stick your underexposed print in your sketchbook and write about what you would do differently next time.

- other people's work: cut out photographs you like from magazines or newspapers, you can also include photocopied examples of artists' work or postcards.

- brainstorming: collect lots of pictures of the same subject matter to see how it has been treated by different photographers. If you are starting a piece of work choose a key word and write down everything you can think of, don't cheat!

- ideas: try to go one step further. For example, if you stick a photograph you like into your book make some notes on the page about why you like it. You don't have to write an essay, just a list of words will help jog your memory.

As at Grange School, this project also used the idea of a group sketch book. It was explained to the students that they could contribute to it as well. It was hoped that this sketch book would provide a model for them, giving them confidence to develop their own ways of using their books. Five students purchased their own sketchbooks, and slowly began to develop a way of working in them, although the amount of material suggests that the students remained uncertain about this unfamiliar way of working. One possible reason for this is the students' lack of confidence in their own ideas, and a reluctance to put down on paper half-formed ideas that can be subject to criticism. This also seemed a factor in the use of the group sketch book. Inspite of prompts the students seemed reluctant to use the group sketch book; partly it seems, because they didn't want to appear 'silly' infront of their class mates. It may be that the culture of assessment in schools under the National Curriculum, combined with peer pressure, discourages the kind of open approaches and risk-taking that are, to a degree, necessary in successful art teaching.

Keywords

landscape
cityscape
viewpoint
horizon
Wythenshawe
environment
island
map
identity
nationality
community

Visiting the Exhibition

The students visited Kate Mellor's exhibition 'Island: The Sea Front', in order to get them thinking about how it might be possible to 'map' an area photographically. They also got an opportunity to meet with the artist and talk to her about her working methods. In order that the students were able to gain maximum benefit from the gallery visit, it was important that some thought went into preparing them. In the first session of the project they were shown a range of different approaches to landscape photography. They were also introduced to Kate Mellor's work and encouraged to think about the construction of the photograph in terms of its intended meanings. The students were encouraged to record their reactions to the image (what questions did it raise? what associations did it have for them?), alongside their interpretation of what was happening in the photograph. [see below]

Reminds me of a holiday in Filey

People appear insignificant

*Empty Bandstand –
is this no longer used*

Pier seems to be broken off

*The Bandstand is blue but the sky
and the sea are not*

Artist: Kate Mellor

*What time of the day?
What season?*

*The crack in the wall continues the line of
fire of the guns the boys are holding*

*This boy is scraping
the wall*

'There is something of the nature of an island in a predisposition towards insularity, as though the physical outline of the land was capable of repeating itself in the shape of a psychological profile. The actual concrete presence of the land itself is a thing of enormous importance in the national psyche'

During the visit they were also asked to think about how presentation and the use of the gallery space might affect the way the audience experienced and made sense of the photographs.

Mapping Our School

In week two the students were split into two groups. Each group was asked to produce a short tape/slide sequence during the lesson. The purpose of the exercise was to introduce photographic skills within the context of a thematic approach. It reproduced on a smaller scale the brief that the students were working on at greater length during the remainder of the project.

Each group was given one camera, a roll of polapan (instant transparency) film, a cassette and cassette player. One group was asked to work to the theme of 'interior', the other group to the theme 'boundary'. This was a valuable exercise for introducing students to a new way of working. If time had permitted, it would have been useful to devote more time to preparation in this way.

Our Wythenshawe

The practical photographic work produced during the rest of the project was of two types:

- photographs taken by students in their own time

- photographic field trips during school time in the local area

The illustrations in this section represent both kinds of photographic activity.

Students were asked to develop an individual piece of work based around the theme. They were given a number of suggestions, and attention was drawn to the need to be specific and not try to take on every aspect of the environment. Students were also introduced to a passage from Soft City by Jonathon Raban to encourage the students to see what they were doing as creating an emotional, rather than purely descriptive, map. The themes they chose included the physical landscape, babies, pollution, graffitti, friends, a comparison between Wythenshawe and Hathersage (in the country), and the airport.

For the field trips they were divided into two groups and asked to select an environment. Again each group was given a one word theme (boundary or interior), which they were asked to interpret. A short discussion took place about possible interpretations. The students were asked to think about the question of literalness and how artists might use symbolism in developing a visual language. Each group of students had a cassette recorder, a compact camera with colour film, an single lens reflex (SLR) camera with black and white film and a video camera, the intention being to generate still images from the video material.

Sarah Lynch

During the last weeks of the project Jane Brake accompanied the students on field trips, because of the problems they were having in generating suitable material on their own. One of the principal difficulties was to balance the need for students to acquire technical photographic skills with the thematic emphasis of the

From group fieldtrip

From group fieldtrip

Alison Buckley

Martin Thorpe

Anthony Nolan

project, given the extremely short timescale. During the field trips the students needed help with all aspects of camera controls and to be given basic guildelines about many other aspects of picture taking: for example, they did not think about varying angles and heights, or about the need to control the background by moving around the subject. It was perhaps expecting a lot to ask them to work independently, without giving this input in a more controlled practical situation.

Conclusions

In retrospect this project was perhaps over-ambitious given the amount of time available, and the interruptions that occurred due to work experience and school trips. The project sought to introduce the students to a new way of working with photography, which placed greater demands on them, particularly with regard to the subject matter and planning of the work. Inevitably, this proved difficult in a situation where many of the students were still coming to grips with basic photographic techniques. Additionally, the pressure of producing work for examination folders - several students said that their main ambition in photography was simply to pass the course - may have the effect of holding back a more productive educational engagement with the medium.

Nevertheless, the students' responses to the project were largely positive. Almost all students said that they enjoyed the project:

"Photography is not like other lessons where you have to sit down for an hour writing. In photography you do practical things."

"I enjoyed the planning, the thoughts and ideas."

The project aimed to give students a chance to investigate and represent aspects of their local environment. It is rewarding to see that students valued this opportunity:

"I have enjoyed getting to know my area better, noticing all the things that haven't been noticed by anyone."

"The project made me think about what Wythenshawe can offer young people."

The students' reflections on the project as an educational experience, and the resulting photographic work provide further support for the argument made throughout this book that photography develops perceptual and investigative skills that are relevant across a wide range of curriculum areas.

Reflections on the Manchester Photography in Education Development Project

In the process of creating a picture it sometimes helps to hold the paper in front of a mirror and in the reversed image see mistakes as well as positive qualities with more clarity, as if the picture was made by someone else, in another time and place. Similarly, I hope that the distancing and objectification of my experience facilitated by the writing of these reflections will generate insights of value to those involved in photography and education.

During the photography development project in the School of Education at Manchester Metropolitan University I had to adopt a number of identities: lecturer, teacher, artist in residence, writer, photographer, project organiser, fund raiser, facilitator, ambassador, employer, and researcher. At times these roles appeared to be in conflict with each other, for example when writing about the work that I myself had done as an artist in residence. However, it was precisely this scope and ambition that made the post such an exciting challenge.

My own experience of a photographic education affected the way I chose and was able to fulfil many of the roles required. It came to represent a norm, and a means of identification with many of the students I encountered, whose experiences appeared similar. My fascination with photography probably started during hours spent at home looking through the catalogue of the 1955 exhibition *The Family of Man*. A photograph of a girl lying naked on a bed of ivy fascinated me. I wanted to know the story, who was she? Was she dead or sleeping? Why was she there? A soldier hugging a crying child conjured up the image of my Grandfather in his air force uniform. This was the only book of photographs I remember seeing during my childhood. Later on I learned to identify the particular view of the world portrayed in this collection of photographs, but for me then it presented a view of a world I had never seen before, which made connections with my own.

As a Fine Art student, I received little formal tuition in photography. At times this lack of technical expertise felt restrictive, at others I enjoyed the creative freedom it allowed and the pleasure of discovering for myself. Despite my lack of formal education in photography, it became central to my practice as an artist. I looked for ways to work with people using visual media; youth work and community arts provided a space to experiment. I also worked on the fringes of press photography, before moving into gallery education. Despite this varied experience, my encounter with art education, in the context of this project, took place from the perspective of a practicing artist. As the post comes to an end I need to rediscover what my own practice may comprise and where it is heading.

II

The development post was formulated with the aim of contributing to several areas: the application of new technologies to the study and practice of photography in education; the effective use of and engagement with galleries, focusing in particular on contemporary art practice; and teacher education. The latter provided the foundation for the post, and determined its location within Manchester Metropolitan University's School of Education. There was a close involvement with teacher education within the school, and in addition to the project work described in the previous chapters of this book, the post included teaching on a range of courses.

However, before exploring the different aspects of the post further, it is worth asking why the post was needed? Why does the profile of the medium need to be raised (as was stated in the job description)? In his introduction, Darren Newbury generously asserts that teachers no longer need to make the case for photography. The importance of photographic and media work, he suggests, has gained national recognition. Whilst this may be true, in the local contexts in which the projects recounted here took place, and in the face of key difficulties expressed by teachers, the arguments for photography did need to be fully rehearsed. The difficulties expressed by teachers can be divided into three main areas: training and expertise, the value of photography in the curriculum, and cost.

Teachers concerns about their lack of training reflects the perception of photography as primarily a technical medium, rather than a creative one which shares many concerns with other art forms, and strives for a balance between considerations of expression and technical expertise. There are insufficient opportunities for art students to engage in in-depth explorations of the medium during their first degrees, and this continues to be the case for those who study for a Post Graduate Certificate in Education. The development post set out to challenge this through the initiation of coursework that was specifically related to photography teaching in schools.

Arguments for the place of photography have been made effectively elsewhere, but there seems to remain an unease about the true place for photography. This may have something to do with the challenge it presents to the traditional architecture of the curriculum, which remains compartmentalized, and divorced from student experience. New technology provides an imperative as well as a fresh opportunity to review this architecture. The work of the post, however, focused mainly on the potential of photography within the art and design curriculum.

Considerations of cost, although antithetical to a pure debate about the educational value of photography, nevertheless impinge on how this subject may be delivered to school students. Access to photography as a primary source in the art room is cheap if not free. There is no reason why the work of photographers should be omitted from the range of material to which students are introduced, particularly when looking at contemporary art practice. The post did not set out specifically to address issues of cost, but all of the work considered here could be realised within normal school budgets, although it would require more preparation and planning time.

III

One of the central themes of this Photography in Education initiative was collaboration. Many arts organisations are having to collaborate with each other as well as with a range of other organisations such as private companies, galleries and educational establishments, in order to survive in a world of contracting funding. Schools are also recognising the benefits of collaborating with other organisations. Working with galleries or universities it is possible for schools to provide their students with opportunities for learning they would not otherwise have, bringing them into contact with working artists. Additionally, collaboration can help with fund raising for particular projects and in providing INSET for teachers. These partnerships can be mutually beneficial. Gallery education departments may be non existent or over stretched, finding little time to keep abreast of developments in the national curriculum. Teachers can work with them by providing this specialist knowledge and have a real impact on the programming and education work of the gallery. The key is imagination, and from the teacher's point of view a sense of students' access to the gallery being a right rather than a privilege. Collaboration will requires set of common, concrete objectives and a mutual recognition of its benefits.

IV

Another irony and challenge lies in the mere fact of a project called photography in education at a time when the notion of photography itself is changing, to become photographies, both chemical and digital. Whilst still referred to as new, the development of digital technology has not occurred in a vacuum or caused a historical rupture with other means of image making. Technological developments have always had an impact on artists work, and artists have in their turn, through experimentation, affected these developments. All the projects in this book in one way or another touch on the question of how artists and students can work with these technologies in the development of their own visual language. 'New technology' has been treated as another tool in the art room, in much the same way as chemical photography. It is the messages, meanings and expressions articulated with this technology that are considered to be of prime importance. An exploration of how artists of all ages may use these technologies in the development of their own visual language needs to take place, with a measured understanding of what each technology does. Like the camera, the computer doesn't do it for you.

The not so new technology of video, although available in many schools, is rarely used creatively in the art room. Video and digital photography may present an opportunity for teachers wishing to include photographic work in their classrooms. Once the initial capital investment has been made, and teacher training needs in this area have been addressed, the production costs as well as the need for specialised facilities can be drastically reduced. In addition health and safety problems associated with the use of chemicals, and water and electricity in close proximity, can be avoided. This is not to suggest that chemical photography will no longer be practised in schools, but that digital technology could engender a growth of photography in schools.

V

What is the relationship between contemporary art practice and what happens in the school art room? What should this relationship be? This is a question to which I have returned many times during the last three years. The issue of contemporary art practice is not only one of the technology employed. Many contemporary artists use photography as an integral part of their practice and not just as a recording medium. The influence of photography is far reaching, and can be traced in the work of many artists who have never touched a camera. Photographers are responding to the development of digital technology, working with moving as well as still imagery generated via film or video. Our understanding of what constitutes art itself has moved beyond the frame into installation, and includes the total concept of how the work must be viewed, and the relationship or involvement of the audience in the production of the work.

In contrast, much of the school art I have seen remains resolutely within the rectangular paper mounts that are so prevalent it is hard to believe that they are not written into the national curriculum. The audience for school art is drawn mainly from the school community: other students, teachers, parents and examiners; only ever in exceptional cases is it presented to a wider artistic community or gallery audience. What should the relationship be between work produced in the school art room and work selected for the Turner Prize, for instance? Teachers have little opportunity to develop as artists themselves, particularly as their workloads increase, and they may themselves feel alienated from developments in contemporary practice. One of the reasons that school art seems unable to move beyond modernism is the difficulty of assessing contemporary work, and the threat it seems to pose to the authority and expertise of the teacher. This may have a lot to do with the underdevelopment of a culture of art criticism which would inform this process in school. Understandably, many teachers find this worrying, particularly in relation to GCSE moderation. Students themselves may well question the relationship between art, as defined by the media or by exhibition curators, and school art. In the words of one student from Ellen Wilkinson School, after a visit to the British Art Show where she saw Damien Hirst's 'Sheep in Formaldyhide': "if I cut up a sheep and put it in a cardboard box would it be

VI

To conclude, I want to say something about the value of the project as a whole. Teachers are the best judges of how useful this research can be in informing classroom practice. I hope that each reader will have found something of relevant to them in practical terms, or perhaps a new perspective on issues that affect their own practice.

There has been a tension running throughout this work between research and practice, the desire to take risks and the need to produce results. Similarly, there is a tension between the desire to be of immediate use to practitioners in the field, and the conventions of academic research. An investment was made, returns were expected. Funding bodies naturally require outcomes which explain or justify the money spent. However strong the commitment to research, which by its nature must be open ended, the products had to look good, to succeed. What was actually learned is often more difficult to measure than the products of that initial encounter, which exist in time, have form, colour, texture, meaning. What the students have learned is less tangible, and may not be evident for years and may not be what was intended at all. But this is what is so exciting: what they make of it all in the end. I am confident that what these young people show to us will not just be a reflection of the picture we drew for them, but seen with their own eyes.

Jane Brake

Select Bibliography

There are a number of key books available for teachers who wish to introduce photography for the first time and for those who are developing further their current practice. Rather than repeat the extensive listings of resources provided both in *Creating Vision* and *Picture My World*, we have chosen simply to refer interested readers to those publications which provide the best introduction.

Binch, Norman & Clive, Sue (1994) *Close Collaborations: art in schools and the wider environment*. London: Arts Council of England.

Hornsby, Jim (1992) *Photography in Art and English*. Tunbridge Wells: Surrey County Council and South East Arts.

Isherwood, Sue, & Stanley, Nick (eds.) (1994) *Creating Vision: Photography and the National Curriculum*. Manchester: Cornerhouse Publications.

Newbury, Darren (1994) *Photography, Art and Media*. Birmingham: Building Sights and the University of Central England.

Walton, Kamina (1995) *Picture My World: Photography in Primary Education*. London: Arts Council of England.